DREW CAREY

OVERCOMING ADVERSITY

DREW CAREY

Ann Graham Gaines

Chelsea House Publishers

Philadelphia

Frontis: Drew Carey and chihuahua "Lady Di" make friends during his appearance at a 1996 celebrity benefit for the Amanda Foundation. The foundation finds homes for hard-to-place animals from the Humane Society.

CHELSEA HOUSE PUBLISHERS

EDITOR IN CHIEF Stephen Reginald
MANAGING EDITOR James D. Gallagher
PRODUCTION MANAGER Pamela Loos
ART DIRECTOR Sara Davis
DIRECTOR OF PHOTOGRAPHY Judy L. Hasday
SENIOR PRODUCTION EDITOR Lisa Chippendale

Staff for **Drew Carey**
SENIOR EDITOR Therese De Angelis
ASSOCIATE ART DIRECTOR Takeshi Takahashi
DESIGNER Keith Trego
PICTURE RESEARCHER Patricia Burns
COVER ILLUSTRATION Gary Ciccarelli
COVER DESIGN Keith Trego

First Printing

1 3 5 7 9 8 6 4 2

Library of Congress Cataloging-in-Publication Data

Gaines, Ann.
Drew Carey / by Ann Graham Gaines.
96 pp.   cm. — (Overcoming adversity)
Includes bibliographical references and index.
Summary: A biography of the stand-up comedian and actor, discussing his sexual abuse as a child, his subsequent battle with depression, and his work in clubs, on television, and in films.

ISBN 0-7910-4942-6 — ISBN 0-7910-4943-4
1. Carey, Drew—Juvenile literature. 2. Comedians—United States—Biography—Juvenile literature. 3. Television actors and actresses—United States—Biography—Juvenile literature. [1. Carey, Drew. 2. Comedians. 3. Actors and actresses.] I. Title. II. Series.
PN2287.C264G35 1998
792.7'028'092—dc21   98-36688
[b]   CIP
                                                             AC

CONTENTS

OVERCOMING ADVERSITY

ON FACING ADVERSITY

James Scott Brady

I GUESS IT'S a long way from a Centralia, Illinois, train yard to the George Washington University Hospital Trauma Unit. My dad was a yardmaster for the old Chicago, Burlington & Quincy Railroad. As a child, I used to get to sit in the engineer's lap and imagine what it was like to drive that train. I guess I always have liked being in the "driver's seat."

Years later, however, my interest turned from driving trains to driving campaigns. In 1979, former Texas governor John Connally hired me as a press secretary in his campaign for the American presidency. We lost the Republican primary to a former Hollywood star named Ronald Reagan. But I managed to jump over to the Reagan campaign. When Reagan was elected in 1980, I was "sitting in the catbird seat," as humorist James Thurber would say—poised to be named presidential press secretary. I held that title throughout the eight years of the Reagan administration. But not without one terrible, extended interruption.

It happened barely two months after the Reagan administration took office. I never even heard the shots. On March 30, 1981, my life went blank in an instant. In an attempt to assassinate President Reagan, John Hinckley Jr. armed himself with a "Saturday night special"—a low-quality, $29 pistol—and shot wildly as our presidential entourage exited a Washington hotel. One of the exploding bullets struck me just above the left eye. It shattered into a couple dozen fragments, some of which penetrated my skull and entered my brain.

The next few months of my life were a nightmare of repeated surgery, broken contact with the outside world, and a variety of medical complications. More than once, I was very close to death.

The next few years were filled with frustrating struggles to function with a paralyzed right side, struggles to speak and communicate.

To people who face and defeat daunting obstacles, "ambition" is not becoming wealthy or famous or winning elections or awards. Words like "ambition" and "achievement" and "success" take on very different meanings. The objective is just to live, to wake up every morning. The goals are not lofty; they are very ordinary.

My own heroes are ordinary folks—but they accomplish extraordinary things because they try. My greatest hero is my wife, Sarah. She's accomplished a lot of things in life, but two stand out. The first has been the way she has cared for me and our son since I was shot. A tremendous tragedy and burden was dropped unexpectedly into her life, totally beyond her control and without justification. She could have given up; instead, she focused her energies on preserving our family and returning our lives to normal as much as possible. Week by week, month by month, year by year, she has not reached for the miraculous, just for the normal. Yet in focusing on the normal, she has helped accomplish the miraculous.

Her other most remarkable accomplishment, to me, has been spearheading the effort to keep guns out of the hands of criminals and children in America. Opponents call her a "gun grabber"; I call her a national hero. And I am not alone.

After a seven-year battle, during which Sarah and I worked tirelessly to educate the public about the need for stronger gun laws, the Brady Bill became law in 1993. It was a victory, achieved in the face of tremendous opposition, that now benefits all Americans. From the time the law took effect through fall 1997, background checks had stopped 173,000 criminals and other high-risk purchasers from buying handguns, and the law has helped to reduce illegal gun trafficking.

Sarah was not pursuing fame, or even recognition. She simply started at one point—when our son, Scott, found a loaded handgun on the seat of a pickup truck and, thinking it was a toy, pointed it at Sarah.

Fortunately, no one was hurt. But seeing a gun nearly bring a second tragedy upon our family, Sarah became determined to do whatever she could to prevent senseless death and injury from guns.

Some people think of Sarah as a powerful political force. To me, she's the person who so many times fed me and helped me dress during my long years of recovery.

Overcoming obstacles is part of life, not just for people who are challenged by disabilities, illnesses, or tragedies, but for all people. No matter what the obstacle—fear, disability, prejudice, grief, or a difficulty that isn't likely to "just go away"—we can all work to make this world a better place.

Drew Carey mugs for the camera in a promotional spot for his new ABC-TV program.

1

A REGULAR GUY

DON'T GET DREW CAREY wrong. He felt both happy and proud when, in the spring of 1995, he finished taping the pilot for *The Drew Carey Show*, the television sitcom that he stars in and created with executive producer Bruce Helford. Carey especially liked the big check he got for his work. (What did he do with the money? Go out and buy a new designer wardrobe? Book a cruise? No, he used it to buy from his mother the Cleveland, Ohio, house he grew up in.)

But though he felt a sense of accomplishment, Drew Carey still wasn't sure whether *The Drew Carey Show* would succeed. A year earlier, in 1994, he'd played a "second banana" role on another situation comedy called *The Good Life*. He had also liked that show and had high hopes for it. While on the set, he'd heard nothing but praise. "All the executives and the director and the network people would say, 'Wow, this is great! This is going to be so funny. This is going to be a big hit. . . . Start buying your mansion now,'" Drew recalls.

But once the show aired, reality hit. *TV Guide*, among other publications, gave it a poor review. Moreover, because few viewers tuned in,

"TV Drew" puts out an office fire on The Drew Carey Show.

the show earned very low Nielsen ratings and was canceled after only a few weeks. (Nielsen is a standard ratings system for television that measures a show's popularity in two ways: first, among all households that own televisions, and second, in "audience shares," or the percentage of households in which televisions are not only turned on, but also tuned to the show. Each point in the ratings represents one percent of television households in the United States, or 980,000 households.)

So, when *The Drew Carey Show* premiered in September 1995, its leading man had a very real fear that he might fall flat on his face. In fact, he could easily visualize the destruction of his entire career. He worried that if this show failed, he might have to support himself by returning to the grueling business of stand-up comedy. Even worse, he would have to get a "real" job (he didn't think of stand-up in that way).

Sadly, this sense of doom was familiar to Drew. He had lived through some tough times, and he sometimes despaired of ever getting ahead. As a young adult, he'd worked scores of dead-end jobs. He already knew what it was like to punch a time clock day after day, yet still scramble to make ends meet.

If *The Drew Carey Show* failed, Carey expected to be held personally accountable, for two reasons. First, he was the star—the sitcom bore his name. Second, he was heavily involved in its development. As a matter of fact, the whole thing had been his idea in the first place.

Drew was part of the stand-up comedy boom that began in the 1980s. It was still going strong in the 1990s, but its nature had changed somewhat. Comedy clubs across America were now forced to compete with the immense popularity of cable TV networks, which viewed comedy shows as an inexpensive means of raising ratings. For a while, it seemed that you could find a stand-up comic on TV almost any time of the day or night.

As a result, paying club customers, realizing that they could see all the free comedy they wanted on television, began staying away from comedy clubs. Despite free tickets and other giveaways from owners, most comedy clubs began losing money during the 1990s, and many of them closed.

Drew Carey is one of a handful of comedians who realized that writing and producing comedy for television was more profitable and steadier work than performing on the comedy circuit. Following the lead of comedians like Bill Cosby (*The Cosby Show*) and Roseanne Barr (*Roseanne*), 1990s comics like Tim Allen, Brett Butler, Ellen DeGeneres, Rosie O'Donnell, Paul Reiser, and Jerry Seinfeld parlayed their talents into writing, producing, and acting for television.

Usually, a successful stand-up comic lands his or her own television show when a studio or production company approaches the comic with an invitation. But Drew

Carey chose a different—and more difficult—route. He didn't want to wait for an offer. He wanted to shape his own destiny and to choose his own "vehicle" or project. What's more, he wanted to pick the executive producer, the man or woman who would ultimately be in charge—the "Show Runner," as he describes the position in his book, *Dirty Jokes and Beer*.

"What I did that was different," Drew recollects, "is that I courted people rather than waiting for the studio to play matchmaker. I had an idea of what I wanted in my producer 'mate.' I knew what kind of show I wanted and the kind of working relationship I wanted with a producer. [So] I met with a bunch of different executive producers. . . . I kept going until I found somebody I really . . . fell in love with." Carey eventually hired Bruce Helford, a veteran TV producer who had written for *Family Ties* and was the executive producer of *Roseanne* during its 1992-93 season.

The first step Carey and Helford had to take was to decide on a concept for the show. Carey not only wanted the show's central character to have his own name, but he also wanted the "TV Drew" to behave very much like himself. He needed to be what he called a "Joe Blow"—or ordinary working man—who doesn't stand out from the pack, someone with whom most viewers could comfortably identify. With this in mind, Carey and Helford created a character who held a small measure of authority but who would only rise high enough in his company to realize just how little power he actually possessed. They gave him the job of assistant personnel director of a department store.

Carey and Helford also decided to make the character a simple man, without a complicated psyche, a single guy who lives alone and hangs out with his best friends. Drew insisted that he be a fundamentally happy individual; he wanted viewers to get the message that people like the TV Drew, who work at jobs as opposed to pursuing careers, can be satisfied with their lives.

Lastly, Drew Carey and Bruce Helford needed a setting.

That was easy. After a trip to Drew's hometown, they set the show in Cleveland, Ohio.

Once ABC-TV announced that it was adding *The Drew Carey Show* to its fall 1995 lineup, Carey had to work even harder to ensure the show's success. He put in long hours helping to write and revise scripts. He rehearsed and rehearsed and rehearsed. He quickly learned to hate dubbing, the process by which sound is added to the visual part of a taped show. He also devoted a lot of time to publicizing the show by appearing in promotional spots, granting interviews, and attending press conferences and parties with members of the television and advertising industries.

After all that, Carey had few doubts about the quality of his show. He still knew, however, that even good TV shows sometimes fail. His biggest fear was that the view-

The cast of The Drew Carey Show *on the set, clockwise from left: Christa Miller, Ryan Stiles, Diedrich Bader, Craig Ferguson, Kathy Kinney, and Drew Carey.*

A fervent fan of his hometown, Drew was elated when Cleveland, Ohio, was named the site of the new Rock & Roll Hall of Fame. He was a guest at the museum's opening in 1995.

ers he was targeting—those who also watched *Roseanne* or *Grace Under Fire*, for example—would either miss the pilot or would dislike it.

Indeed, *The Drew Carey Show* wasn't an immediate hit. A few reviewers praised the premiere episode, and the show was included on lists of new shows to watch. But for the most part it was panned. Critics called it an unsuccessful clone of the popular sitcom *Friends*, whose premise centers around a cast of mostly unmarried buddies. In fact, the "unmarried buddies" format was widely imitated during the 1990s. Jurgen Wolff, a television insider, has called this period the era of the "singles" sitcom. Earlier TV series often revolved around a family or a group of colleagues. But because Carey was aiming for a different audience, such reviews dimmed his hope that his might be recognized as a show in the working-class vein.

A *TV Guide* critic called the show's scripting "formulaic" (predictable) and thought the jokes fell flat. Another reviewer pointed out that Carey is heavy, Kate (Christa Miller) is tomboyish, and Oswald and Lewis (Diedrich Bader and Ryan Stiles) are funny but not classically handsome. He wondered, rather unkindly, whether anyone would want to watch a show about unattractive people.

Some critics were especially harsh about Carey's acting skills; one called him "wooden." Even an influential advertising agency executive, who helps companies decide where to place their commercials, said that *The Drew Carey Show* lacked an "acceptable lead" (or star), and that it lacked a theme.

By the time the first season ended, however, the real Drew Carey felt satisfied with the work he had done. The show remained true to his vision. His character was still "everyman." And to Drew's delight, the residents of Cleveland were very pleased with him. They clearly appreciated the great affection he feels for his hometown. Most of all, Drew believed that the show was improving and getting funnier each week.

The Drew Carey Show finished its first season ranked 44th on the TV ratings charts. It had made a respectable, if not brilliant, showing, and ABC renewed it for another season. It was then, he wrote in his book, that he began to realize that he was going to earn what he calls "ridiculous" money. Carey celebrated by buying another house—this time in Los Angeles, California—and a large-screen television. Later, he sprang for a new accordion.

Carey's confidence ultimately proved well placed. In its second year, *The Drew Carey Show* rose in the Nielsen ratings to become a Top 20 hit. Every week, more than 10 million households tuned in. And somewhere along the way, Drew Carey himself became famous. By now, most Americans easily recognize him in the caricature that was commissioned for his show: a line drawing consisting of a cartoonish pair of big black glasses, a pair of twinkling eyes, a crewcut, and a tie.

Unlike many other celebrities who have achieved fame and fortune, Drew Carey has remained true to himself. His personality hasn't changed. He resists refinement. And he never forgets where he came from. He continues to live, as much as possible, the way he always has, without most of the trappings of fame. Carey believes that it's the only way to stay funny and to continue to entertain people who are just like him. "How can anyone maintain a good sense of humor and talk about things [that] regular people relate to," he asks, "if you live so vastly differently from the way they do?"

Drew Carey knows what being a celebrity means. He won a People's Choice Award. He is frequently invited to star-studded events. No fewer than a dozen websites are devoted to him or to *The Drew Carey Show*. He's even written a popular book. But at heart, he's still a regular guy. Sure, he likes the money, the recognition, and the special treatment that comes with stardom. But ultimately, he says, "I'm only a comedian in a sitcom, for crying out loud."

Carey takes off his trademark suit and tie for a relaxed evening out. Drew says that his appearance and demeanor are similar to that of his father, Lewis Carey, who died when Drew was eight years old. "I still have very few memories of him when he wasn't sick," he recalls in his book, Dirty Jokes and Beer.

2

A CHIP OFF
THE OLD BLOCK

DREW ALLISON CAREY was born in Cleveland, Ohio, on May 23, 1958, the third of three sons born to Lewis and Beulah Carey. By the time he was born, his parents were both in their late thirties. Because the boys were born six years apart from one another, Drew and his brothers, Neal and Roger, didn't spend much time together while growing up. When Drew entered first grade, for example, Roger was in seventh grade and Neal had already graduated from high school.

Drew's physical appearance today is strikingly similar to that of his father at the same age. Drew has held onto his dad's employee I.D. card for more than 30 years, in part to show people how much like his father he really is. Like Drew, Lewis was a relatively short man, standing 5' 7", and he had a broad, square face. Lewis Carey was also a rather conservative dresser, like most of the middle-class men of his day. Even when playing cards with friends at the local lodge, Lewis wore a dark suit, a starched white shirt, and a skinny tie. In photos from this period he looks very much like Drew does today in his stand-up act and on television.

Lewis Carey worked as a draftsman for General Motors, creating mechanical drawings for engineers. In the mid-1960s, many Americans would have considered this a very desirable job. As automobiles became more affordable after World War II, Americans began buying them in record numbers: 58 million, virtually all of them American-made, in the 1950s alone. American-built cars were a source of great pride to the nation during this period. Thanks to labor unions, U.S. car manufacturers paid their workers well and provided many benefits. Before Drew was born, Lewis Carey had saved enough to buy a small "starter" home in the Old Brooklyn section of Cleveland.

The residents of Old Brooklyn were predominantly descendants of immigrants from Ireland, Poland, and Italy. Most of the men held "blue-collar" jobs in factories, and most of the women were housewives. Although few could afford luxuries like vacations, the area was a safe and pleasant place to raise children, and the Carey boys had many friends their age.

Drew grew up during the 1960s, a turbulent time in the United States. Across the nation, the civil rights movement was slowly establishing political, social, and economic equality for African Americans and other minorities. As the decade wore on, the country also struggled with its increasing involvement in the Vietnam War. On college campuses, a youth movement arose that challenged the traditional beliefs and values of previous generations.

But the Carey family seems to have remained largely unaffected by these social and political upheavals. In Cleveland, polka music still received as much radio air play as rock and roll did. Drew's earliest years were stable and happy. In a recent interview, he described this insular life as positive in some ways. "In my family," he said, "we didn't think much past next winter. My friends and I didn't think beyond next week. We were clueless, but we had a no-bull approach to life."

In some ways, Cleveland can be a difficult place to live. Because of its location on Lake Erie, winters are often bit-

terly cold. Snow arrives early and sometimes lasts well into baseball season in the spring. Cleveland summers can also be unpleasant because of the heat and humidity generated by air currents coming off of Lake Erie.

In the 1960s, most Americans would have considered Cleveland the last place they wanted to live. It had a reputation as a dirty, decaying, industrial town. It didn't help matters when the Cuyahoga River, which feeds into Lake Erie at Cleveland, caught fire because it was so heavily contaminated by pollutants. A great deal has changed since then. Today, Cleveland calls itself the New All-American City; the *Places Rated Almanac* ranks it among the nicest places in the nation to live.

Drew Carey has nothing but fond words for his hometown, even for its weather. "I miss Cleveland in the win-

Soldiers carry an injured Marine to safety in Vietnam, 1967. The controversy and anguish over America's involvement in the Vietnam War seemed to have little effect on the residents of the Cleveland neighborhood where Drew Carey grew up. "[W]e were clueless, but we had a no-bull approach to life," he says.

Residents dig out from a blizzard in Cleveland, Ohio, 1962. Despite its harsh weather, Drew Carey has only praise for his hometown.

ter," he said while living in Los Angeles. "Not the bitter cold days when every breath threatens to shatter your lungs like a hammer taken to a pane of glass; but the crisp, clear days when you can hear the crunch of the snow under every step, and all the air around you seems clean and fresh. Like God made it that day just for you." Other members of the Carey family have stayed close to their Cleveland roots. Beulah Carey still lives in the area, and Drew's brother Roger lives in the city.

Drew has warm recollections of his early childhood. After church on Sundays, the Careys would all gather around the television to watch their favorite local variety show. One of Drew's favorite memories is of sitting in the kitchen watching his usually hardworking father ham it up, like the performers in the variety show. Sometimes, Lewis would even break into an impromptu tap dance.

Such memories of his dad are, unfortunately, very few. Drew can't remember playing catch with his father or going to ball games with him, although he's sure that his father wanted to do these things. But Lewis Carey ran out of time. While Drew was still in elementary school, his father had several heart attacks, and then he developed brain cancer.

Drew was just eight years old when Lewis Carey died at age 45. In his book, Drew described his memories of that painful time. His father's death was devastating, but it was not unexpected:

> He'd been in and out of Deaconess Hospital (the same hospital I was born in) ever since I could remember, and I still have very few memories of him when he wasn't sick.
>
> He had blood clots in his legs, a couple of strokes, a heart attack or two. . . . [T]hen a brain tumor finally got to him. When I was seven, he had an eye removed in an effort to get at the tumor. I thought it was cool because he wore a patch. He even let me look into the socket once, and showed me how he could breathe through the hole where his eye used to be.
>
> Those are the kinds of memories I have of my old man. I remember ambulances taking him away from the house. I remember seeing him in the hospital. . . . I remember him coming home from the hospital. I remember the funeral.

In the years following the death of his father, Drew suffered from bouts of severe depression stemming not only from losing his father, but also from the fact that at nine years old, he was sexually molested. He revealed this abuse for the first time in *Dirty Jokes and Beer*. "I didn't tell anyone that it happened," he wrote. Not even members of his family knew about it:

> I was raised in a time [when] everyone thought that sex was dirty, and nobody talked about it, ever. Not to a nine-year-old anyway. . . . So I didn't [talk about it either]. Never told a therapist, or a teacher, or a minister, or a family member. All my life I lived with it buried inside me. . . . Every once

in a while it would come up in my mind, but I would quickly force it back down, because somehow I knew it would make me take an honest look at how badly certain things in my life had been [messed] up because of it.

Until the death of her husband, Beulah Carey had been a stay-at-home mom. Now solely responsible for her three children, she took a job as a keypunch operator. Overwhelmed by her own situation, Beulah may not have realized how deeply troubled her youngest son was. In *Home Brewed: the Drew Carey Story*, author Kathleen Tracy claims that at one point Drew became so concerned about his own mental health that he asked his mother to find him psychiatric help—a very unusual request from a child, and one that most people in Old Brooklyn would never have considered. His mother promised Drew that she would look into it, Tracy says, but she never found the time to do so.

Nevertheless, Drew's devotion to his mother is evident in *Dirty Jokes and Beer*, which is filled with bantering and funny stories. The book's few serious words are about Beulah. "She [has] stood by me through [everything], supporting me spiritually and financially, believing in me, and loving me," Drew wrote. "And I love her. More than words can say."

Aside from saying that the abuser was not a relative, Carey will never publicly discuss the details of his abuse. In his book he says that the long process of recovering from his trauma "could take up an entire book of its own," yet he refuses to make his painful experience the subject of celebrity interviews and articles. "[A]fter this book is done," Carey wrote, "I don't want to talk about it in public ever again. I don't want to make a living off [of] it."

Although Drew does not wish to dwell on the specifics of his own ordeal, he acknowledges that keeping sexual abuse a secret harms its victims psychologically. He pleads with those who may have suffered similar experiences to seek help. "A therapist, a book, anything to start a healing process so that you can enjoy your life more.

There's a lot of guilt and self-hate that results from being sexually abused or molested," Drew admits. "You don't need to live with it for the rest of your life."

Carey says that one of the ways in which he has come to terms with his own experience has been to read widely on the subject. He believes this has helped him "figure out how to get rid of all the negative feelings about myself that came with [being abused]." In fact, this is Carey's favorite way to work through problems of all kinds. He loves to read. Often, when faced with a difficult situation, Drew's first step is to visit a library or bookstore for information and advice about whatever is on his mind.

Growing up without his father was very difficult for Drew, but he learned that staying busy and pursuing his own interests made his father's absence easier to bear. Music was one of Drew's greatest passions. He began taking accordion lessons in first grade. Later, he learned to play the trumpet, which he continued through college. He also sang in his church choir. And Drew landed a role as Frederick, the pirate apprentice, in Mooney Junior High School's production of Gilbert and Sullivan's comic opera *The Pirates of Penzance*. It seemed that he had inherited his father's penchant for entertainment.

"Even though he wasn't all that outgoing, Drew was a born ham," says one friend. "He thinks nothing about getting in front of people singing or dancing. Even as a gawky teenager, he just went for it, and he just ate up the applause. . . . It was his first taste of having an audience in his hand, and he liked it a lot." But Drew simply thought of the experience as fun; he didn't yet harbor any serious ambition to become an actor.

Outside of school, Drew spent most of his time alone. The Carey house was empty by the time he came home each day, so he would often stop off at the local library or record store on the way. He remembers that he also spent a lot of time watching TV, especially cartoons. On days when school was canceled because of snow, he might watch TV

Drew brings his love for music and entertaining to his own TV program and to his celebrity appearances. He is pictured here as the host of the 25th Annual American Music Awards in January 1998.

all day. "There was never anything good on, but I didn't care," Drew remembers. "I watched reruns of *The Beverly Hillbillies*, *Bewitched*, *Branded*, and every game show I could find. . . . Back then, if I could've jumped into the TV and lived in any TV show, it would've been *The Beverly Hillbillies*. Man, I'd rule that house. Granny making me vittles, Jethro running my errands, and Ellie Mae . . . oh, sweet Ellie Mae."

Though he's somewhat stout today, Drew was a skinny kid in junior high and he remained that way into adulthood. Family snapshots show him with long, blonde hair, already wearing thick glasses. And, in keeping with the fashion of the early 1970s, he sported polyester shirts and flared pants. His mother tormented him, he says, by making him wear a "nerdy" snowsuit and giant boots in the winter, when the coolest kids were wearing denim jackets and sneakers ("Frostbite was the ultimate status symbol," he jokes).

The teenaged Drew spent a lot of free time playing games. One game he especially liked was called Dungeons & Dragons, a role-playing fantasy game that can be played intermittently for weeks at a time (personal computers and video games had yet to be invented). He was a member of the high school wrestling team, though he was apparently not very good, and he was a trumpet player in the school marching band. Drew jokes that "the babes were all over him" when he wore his band uniform. "I looked like an army colonel holding a trumpet," he laughs. For a time, he also played the accordion in a polka band, but his mother made him quit when the band started getting offers to play in bars.

Drew also liked to read joke books, and he listened to comedy records (in the days before CDs), trying to imitate the comedians' timing and delivery. In school, he gained a reputation as class clown, but he never believed that he was very funny:

> I was always the joker . . . but I always thought my friends were funnier, so I tried to make myself funnier by listening to different comedians and knowing lots of jokes. I'd listen to the morning radio jokes and mimic the[m] for my friends. I thought it would make people like me more.

Though he was never wildly popular, Drew does have a number of high school friends with whom he is still in touch.

In his junior year of high school, Drew Carey decided that he had no good reason to stay in school for another year. He wanted to graduate early. After all, he reasoned, he'd never been a very serious student, and he'd never had a favorite teacher or academic subject. He must have been bright enough, however, for he was able to skip his senior year. That summer, he took a senior English course—the

The James Ford Rhodes High School in Cleveland. Impatient with his studies, Drew Carey skipped his senior year here and enrolled in Kent State University.

last requirement for graduation—and received his diploma.

Beulah Carey could not afford to send Drew to a private college, so he requested tuition grants and student loans from state-funded Kent State University, a huge school in Ashtabula, Ohio.

If Drew couldn't wait to finish high school, why did he want to attend college? "No reason," he claims in *Dirty Jokes and Beer*. "I just figured I should go to college, so I went." He had no particular interests. He had no career goals. He wasn't even sure what subject to major in. "I just knew that after high school, that's where people usually went."

Carey claims that this is the way he's made many decisions about his life. But he also adds that "making important life decisions like that has backfired on me." The only successes he's had, he asserts, are those that he has not only needed and wanted but has also planned carefully.

As a college-bound teenager, Drew Carey may not have known what he wanted to do with his life, but he knew what he did not want to do. He didn't want to end up as just another "working stiff" in a factory somewhere. He wanted something different and unusual out of life; he just didn't yet know what it was.

Drew speaks about his poor college grades and how depression affected his life during a Mood Disorders Symposium at Johns Hopkins Medical Center in April 1996. "God gave me a second and third chance to accept being alive and imperfect," Carey says in his book. "[T]hat's what I'm going to be: Alive—taking chances, making mistakes, and enjoying every minute of it."

3

DESPAIR AND DETERMINATION

WHEN HE ARRIVED at Kent State University, Drew Carey was, in many ways, a naive teen. He didn't have much experience dating girls. He had never used or abused drugs or alcohol. And he wasn't sure why he was attending college anyway. Today, Drew acknowledges that graduating early from high school was a terrible mistake. At 17, he was too young and immature for college; he now believes that he would have greatly benefited from spending another year in high school.

Kent State University was an enormous and well-known school. Five years earlier, in 1970, it had drawn the attention of the entire country when four students who were protesting America's presence in the Vietnam War were killed by National Guardsmen sent to quell the uprising.

Three thousand armed militiamen had been stationed on campus on May 3, 1970. The next day, 600 students staged a demonstration protesting the escalation of the war. The peaceful event, devoted to speeches and folk songs, was interrupted by the National Guard, who began to march on the protesters. The atmosphere grew more tense.

A student waves a black flag as he faces National Guardsmen on the campus of Kent State University on May 4, 1970. Shortly after this photograph was taken, the student was shot and wounded when guardsmen opened fire on protesters.

Suddenly, an unknown person threw a rock, and protesters began shouting. Armed with bayoneted rifles, Guardsmen tossed tear gas canisters into the crowd in an attempt to disperse the protesters. When the students tried to run, some of the Guardsmen panicked and opened fire on them. Within 15 seconds, they had killed four people and wounded 11 others. The situation seemed even more tragic when an investigation revealed that two of the victims were bystanders, merely passing by on their way to lunch.

The killings at Kent State had occurred almost at the end of the antiwar movement of the 1960s and early 1970s, and the Vietnam War ended—at least for America—in 1974. Though hippie fashions and behavior were still mildly popular for a few years afterward, by the time Drew Carey arrived at Kent State the era of student protest was over.

At college, Drew Carey joined the marching band and the "pep band," which performed at basketball games. One of his first moves, though, was joining a fraternity. It was simply the "thing to do" when a person went to college, Drew remembers thinking. The decision would have far-reaching consequences for the young man away from home for the first time.

Even though he was legally too young to drink, Carey made the rounds of keg parties at campus fraternity houses during "rush week," a period where potential initiates and fraternity members get a chance to size one another up. At one of the fraternity houses, Delta Tau Delta, Drew was questioned about his hobbies, and he began talking about his love of board games. But he mistook the frat brother's polite interest as real enthusiasm and arrived a week later for another party carrying a stack of games under his arm. Drew's hosts started to scoff at him, but changed their minds and sat down to play instead. They had become friends.

Thus Drew pledged Delta Tau Delta, moving out of his dormitory and into the fraternity house. During his freshman year, he went through some important rites of passage. Away from home, without the supervision of his mother and the unspoken code of conduct of conservative Old Brooklyn, Drew's behavior changed drastically.

In addition to drinking, he had sex for the first time. In an era when the threat of AIDS did not exist, Drew became preoccupied with dating, and had sex with a number of female students. He also began experimenting with illegal drugs.

Drew's mother would have been appalled to see the change in her son. But his fraternity brothers were not seeing the "real" Drew, either. To them, their new friend was the ultimate party guy. Though he did attend some classes and switched majors several times in an attempt to discover what kind of career he wanted, none of the courses he took held his attention for very long. He knew he was squandering a good opportunity, and he began to feel worthless and irritable.

In addition, Drew's complex feelings about his father's death and about his sexual abuse had been gnawing at him. It is normal and healthy to feel anger toward a deceased parent, even years afterward. But Drew had kept those emotions to himself for a long time. He knew he was angry, but he didn't know why. The more adrift he felt, the more he turned to drinking and playing board games to avoid confronting his edginess and his rage.

To his friends, Drew seemed happy enough, despite his occasional angry outbursts. But Drew's emotional problems were coming to a head. One night, in the midst of a frat party, Drew looked around the room and saw clearly how shallow and unsatisfying his life had become. "Everyone was having such a good time, I couldn't stand it," he remembers. "I got so mad, I could barely control my rage." He returned to his room and swallowed a huge handful of sleeping pills, intent on killing himself.

Almost immediately, however, he had a change of heart. He suddenly became so afraid of going to hell after his death that he called his fraternity brothers and told them what he had done. They rushed him to a nearby health center, where medics gave him ipecac (a substance that induces vomiting) to help him empty his stomach.

Today, most colleges and universities spend a great deal of time and money trying to help students with emotional difficulties before they resort to such tragic measures. But after Drew's suicide attempt, neither the health center nor Delta Tau Delta's house mother arranged follow-up visits

Although Drew Carey spent five years at Kent State (shown here) without graduating, he now advises other kids to "study, learn, find a major" while in college.

for him with a psychiatrist or counselor. Though Drew still felt deeply troubled, he simply resumed his previous behavior. He apparently experienced no real breakthrough.

But Carey's lack of study and his classroom absences eventually caught up with him. Twice, he was academically dismissed—expelled—for poor grades. At one point his grade-point average fell to 0.5 (out of 4.0), lower than a D. He failed at least half of his classes. Finally in 1980, after five years, he left without earning a degree. He hadn't even declared a major.

One of the many glittering casinos in Las Vegas, Nevada. Tantalized by the city's glamour, Drew moved there from Ohio in 1980.

In the entire time that Carey attended Kent State University, he had never decided what he ultimately wanted to do or be. Although he had great fun with his fraternity brothers, he now regrets that he doesn't have a college degree. In *Home Brewed*, Drew shares his thoughts about the importance of making the most of such opportunities:

> I know what I should have done to graduate, and my advice to some guy sitting around drinking beer all night instead of studying would be . . . study, learn, find a major. Be there to be there or get out; [otherwise] you're better off saving your money.

Now, Carey says, "I work so hard. Society is so credential-oriented. . . . I've always felt I have to prove I'm not stupid, since I never got my degree." But he adds that it's important to be comfortable with who you are and what you can do. "You have to let the past go and be whatever you want to be," Carey says.

In 1980, the Kent State dropout returned to Cleveland and moved back into his mother's house, but he was unable to find any rewarding work. Mostly, he waited on tables in restaurants. He did devote a lot of time to following local professional sports, including the Cleveland Browns football team and the Cleveland Indians baseball team. "Man, I'm telling you, it's so hard being a sports fan in Cleveland," he jokes. For years, both teams performed poorly, and being a die-hard fan of such teams did little to cheer him up.

Drew stayed in Cleveland only a few months before he left home again, this time for Las Vegas, Nevada. He had taken a bus trip across the country to visit his brother Neal, who lived in California, and in the short time the bus had stopped in Las Vegas, Drew had been captivated.

Today, the city of Las Vegas has established a reputation as a family vacation spot. In 1980, however, it was still strictly a place for adults who wanted to escape their everyday lives. The sheer number of all-night casinos and strip clubs in the area earned it the nickname "Sin City."

At first, Drew Carey enjoyed Las Vegas. He liked the fact that most of the glamorous casinos and other businesses on brightly lit Las Vegas Boulevard (often called the "Strip") were open night and day. He often gambled at the casinos himself. But Drew was still in turmoil, even though he seemed fine on the surface. "I was in great health," Carey remembers of this period in his life. "I had great friends, but I hated myself so much. I had a really bad self-image. I was ugly. I just didn't like myself and nothing was good enough. I remember thinking, 'All my friends have [steady] jobs now. They're succeeding, but what am I doing?'"

In Las Vegas, just as in Cleveland, Carey could find only dead-end jobs. He worked as a bank teller, then got a second job waiting on tables at a Denny's restaurant. His "home" was a cheap, run-down motel room. And his gambling habit became a serious problem. At one point, he lost all of his rent money and ended up living in his car. Drew began to feel the way he had at Kent State—as though he just couldn't do anything right.

Dale Carnegie, author of one of the many self-help books Drew Carey consulted while he was recovering from his second suicide attempt.

Then one night, he came out of the building where he worked and discovered that his car had been stolen. It was a huge blow. Now he had nowhere to live. Even though the theft was random, he felt as if it was one more piece of evidence that he "wasn't a good enough person." He felt like such a failure that he again attempted suicide. "I had been getting just more and more depressed until finally, I didn't see anything at the end of the tunnel: no light, no food, no love—nothing," Carey remembers. So he swallowed a handful of sleeping pills.

Once again, Drew Carey's will to live must have been stronger than his wish to die. Immediately after taking the pills he called some friends, who got him medical help before the drug could take effect.

This time, Drew knew that he couldn't shrug off his depression and feelings of worthlessness. Instead, he let his family know that he was in serious trouble. The Careys rallied around him. His brother Roger sent him enough money to buy a bus ticket to his mother's home in Cleveland. His family's loving reaction to his situation made him realize that he was a worthwhile person and that people truly cared about him.

But Drew also knew that he had to do something for himself. While staying in Cleveland, he began reading self-help books by authors like Dale Carnegie, Wayne Dyer, and Og Mandino. These books were filled with advice about how to see yourself in a positive light. They emphasized that each person has the power to change his or her life if they choose to. Carey began to understand that the only way he could turn his life around was by learning to like himself. And the way to do that was to find something that made him feel as though he had some purpose in the world.

In 1980, a few months after his suicide attempt, a much improved Drew Carey set off for an extended visit with Neal, who had moved to Mission Viejo, California, several years earlier. Mission Viejo is located near San Diego, the site of both the U.S. Navy's Training Command for the Pacific fleet and a U.S. Marine Corps Recruit Depot.

One day, Drew was exploring San Diego when he passed a recruiting office and decided to learn more about the U.S. military. Once inside, he read some of the material provided for potential recruits, and he began to seriously consider becoming a member of the U.S. Naval Reserves.

Military reservists are trained members of the nation's armed forces who are not on full-time active duty but are always available in emergencies, including war, civil disturbances, and natural disasters such as floods and earthquakes. The president of the United States, and in some

U.S. Marine Corps recruits during basic training exercises near San Diego, California, where Drew Carey completed his training in 1980.

cases state governors, have the authority to order reservists into service in these situations.

While Drew was looking over the material in the office lobby, a Marine Corps recruiter asked him to stop by his office before he left the building. "It was an easy choice after that," he says of his decision to join the U.S. Marine Corps Reserve. "The marine office was neat as a pin with every paper straightened on every single desk. . . . The marines were always sitting up straight and ready to go."

What Drew Carey liked most about becoming a marine reservist was that the Marine Corps promised to give back to its soldiers just as much as it asked of them. One brochure promised that "for all an individual gives, they get even more in return: training, good pay, benefits, and a chance to bring his or her level of physical and mental fitness to its highest level." It was just what Drew Carey had been seeking: a way not only to improve his health and learn discipline, but also to gain self-respect.

As a reservist, Drew Carey was committed to spending one weekend each month and two weeks each year training with the local Marine Reserve Unit. But first, he was required to attend boot camp, just like all other recruits. He did not relish the idea. He'd heard stories about boot camp trainees enduring a great deal of physical abuse. But in *Dirty Jokes and Beer*, he quips that his initial fear soon gave way to sheer exhaustion:

> You only wish they would beat you. Then at least it would be over with and you could get on with your training day.
>
> But no. Instead it was fingertip push-ups until your arms collapsed, "mountain climbers" until you were ready to pass out, or sit-ups until you were ready to puke. Another favorite game was when they would have you rolling around in a dusty pit while the sweat poured off your face and made the dirt and sand stick to [you] like a thousand annoying bugs. But they never hit you. That would've been too kind.

When he entered boot camp, Drew Carey was an out-of-shape, confused kid who had spent years overindulging in beer. Surviving the ordeal became a source of personal pride for Drew and provided a much-needed boost to his self-esteem. His tour of duty lasted six years; by the time he was finished, he had received perfect scores on his physical fitness tests, and he had begun attending college again. "The things I learned in the Marine Corps have stayed with me to this day," he says in his book. "I hate being late, I'm very organized, and I'm not afraid to take responsibility for my own actions, just to name a few." And, he adds drolly, "You could scream at me at the top of your lungs and call me all the names you want. It wouldn't even faze me."

Carey credits the Marine Corps with having helped him to find a focus for his life. It also helped toughen him emotionally, making him feel less concerned about other people's opinions of him and more positive about his own ability to cope with difficult situations. Now, he says, "I let myself do whatever I want, with whomever I want, whenever I want, and don't care if anybody likes it or not. . . . I take more chances."

Carey makes it clear, however, that he's not saying he isn't responsible for his own actions. Rather, he says, it's important to know what you want and how to get it without worrying too much about how other people might react. And as a celebrity, Drew also tries not to worry about how the media react. "I don't have to try to hide what the press calls 'my wild side' because I don't care who knows," he asserts.

The Marine Corps helped Carey realize who he was and what he wanted, but so did his two brushes with death. "I should be dead by now," he says. "But because I'm not, and because God gave me a second and third chance to accept being alive and imperfect, that's what I'm going to be: Alive—taking chances, making mistakes, and enjoying every minute of it."

When he wasn't studying, working, or serving time in the Marines, Drew Carey avidly read books. He still loves to read in his free time, sometimes just for pleasure but also for information and advice. During his time in the Marine Corps Reserve, he continued to read scores of self-help books. In fact, he believes that, more than anything or anyone else, the advice he found there helped him become successful. In *Dirty Jokes and Beer*, he extends thanks to no fewer than 10 authors of self-help volumes, and he makes clear that there were many others. "These books have taught me to set goals, to believe in myself, to make an honest assessment of my abilities, how to stay focused on things that are important to me . . . so many good things that I can't list them all here," Carey wrote.

Drew Carey was by no means a bookworm. Although he read constantly and enjoyed spending time alone, he was—and is—a gregarious person who has been fortunate enough to form strong and lasting friendships. While he served in the Marine Corps Reserve and took college courses, he also held a series of jobs, including waiting tables, because he enjoyed interacting with people.

By 1985, Drew Carey had returned to Cleveland. This time, living in his hometown proved to be good for him. Although he still didn't know what kind of career he wanted, he was no longer simply waiting for something to come along; instead, he was preparing himself for whatever the future might hold. He still waited tables, wherever he could get work, but thanks to his time in the Marine Corps Reserve and his own self-help program, his attitude toward life had changed. He began to set goals for himself. And for the first time, he started to look for a career—a line of work that offered more than just money for paying his bills and buying beer.

Drew Carey in a lighthearted moment.

4

FUNNY MAN

DREW CAREY MAY have been on the road to success in 1985, but it was anything but smooth. One day, after getting into a huge fight with the owner and manager of the restaurant where he worked, he was fired. Now he had to look for yet another job.

Around that time, a friend who was a disc jockey at a Connecticut radio station and knew Drew's sense of humor asked Drew if he'd like to write jokes for his morning program. The pay was modest: "Ten or twenty bucks, something like that," Drew recalls. It sounded so easy. "I thought, 'Wow, I can make like a hundred bucks a week off this guy.'"

The deejay may have made the offer on the spur of the moment, but Carey took it seriously. He was determined to do the job well. Instead of simply writing down the jokes he liked to tell his friends, he decided to do some research on how to write successful comedy. To do so he returned to one of his favorite boyhood haunts: the Cleveland Public Library. There he found a book by Brad Ashton called *How to Write Comedy*. "I pored over that book, taking notes and practically memorizing it, and taught myself how to write jokes," Drew remembers. In

November of that year, he sent his first batch of jokes to his deejay friend.

Drew Carey has never been a great follower of tradition. He doesn't like birthday celebrations, and he claims to deplore Christmas; he devotes an entire chapter of *Dirty Jokes and Beer* to his explanation of why he refuses to celebrate the holiday. But as New Year's Day, 1986, approached, Carey decided to follow tradition and make a resolution. He'd begun to realize that he wanted to pursue his lifelong interest in comedy, and he set out to see whether he could make a living being funny.

Drew promised himself that in 1986 he'd take a shot at doing stand-up comedy. First, he needed to try his jokes on a live audience. He started by participating in an amateur "open-mike" night at a local comedy club.

Ten years earlier, Drew Carey wouldn't have been able to do what he did. Not because he lacked talent, but because he would have been unable to find a comedy club in or near Cleveland, Ohio. Such establishments simply didn't exist, except in large East and West Coast cities like New York and Los Angeles.

Beginning in the 1930s, the most popular venue for comedians was the resort hotels of the Catskill Mountains, near New York City. The best comics—Henny Youngman and Bob Hope, for example—were also booked into nightclubs. Around the same period, radio shows frequently featured comedians as well.

Not until the 1960s, however, did clubs specifically devoted to comedy appear in the United States. The first, called the Improvisation Cafe, opened in New York City's Greenwich Village in 1963. In fact, the term "stand-up" wasn't coined until about 1966—eight years after Drew Carey was born.

The business of comedy underwent a revolution in 1975, when the wildly popular late-night show *Saturday Night Live* debuted on television. The same year, a new cable network called Home Box Office (HBO) broadcast

Legendary comic Henny Youngman (center) with fellow performers at New York's Copacabana, 1950. Clubs devoted specifically to comedy routines did not appear in America until the late 1960s and early 1970s.

its first live comedy performance, featuring Robert Klein. Television boosted stand-up comedy's popularity, and before long, live clubs such as the Improv in New York and the Comedy Store in Los Angeles were flourishing.

While such clubs were drawing huge crowds, however, the comics who entertained them went unpaid. Owners like Bud and Silver Friedman of the Improv and Mitzi Shore of the Comedy Store believed that since they were helping aspiring comedians by providing a "training ground" for them, it was not necessary to compensate them for their work. In 1979, however, a group of comics calling themselves "Comedians for Compensation" went on strike at the Comedy Store, demanding payment for

Although he produces and stars in a popular TV sitcom, Drew Carey still returns to his first love, stand-up comedy, whenever he has time. He has also earned a reputation for helping aspiring young stand-up comedians by encouraging them and giving them advice on improving their acts.

their work. After a bitter struggle, Mitzi Shore agreed to pay comics a minimum of $25 per set. The L.A. Improv, opened by Bud Friedman, quickly followed suit. And under threat of a similar strike, New York City clubs also agreed to pay their talent.

Though club owners initially feared that this new expense would erode their profits, the comedy business thrived and expanded. Before long, promoters began hiring young comics for "showcase" performances in small bars, dance halls, and other out-of-the-way venues, and the trend spread inward from the East and West Coasts. Around the same time, cable TV networks such as HBO and Showtime discovered that live or taped stand-up comedy acts provided inexpensive and popular entertainment programs. By 1986, approximately 300 paying showcases had sprung up across the country.

That, of course, was precisely when Drew Carey entered the "comedy market." His first appearance onstage, during open-mike night at a Cleveland comedy club, lasted about five minutes. In his words, he "totally bombed." But those five minutes were all he needed. His failure didn't deter him. "[A]fter that, there was no turning back. I knew this was something I could be good at." He kept participating in amateur nights, which were usually held on slow nights like Mondays, Tuesdays, or Wednesdays, when fewer people were in the audience.

In April 1986, just four months after his first appearance onstage, Drew Carey got a job as an emcee, the announcer who introduces other comics. This was a fairly important position, and often paid more than a stand-up gig itself. Carey was hired, at $100 a week, to open nine shows with 10 minutes of his own material.

But Drew Carey's problems weren't over yet. Audiences aren't always kind to comics they don't like or don't think are funny. Sometimes comics are even heckled off the stage. And Drew still wasn't feeling completely sure of himself. Late in the summer of 1986, he was in the middle of his act when he decided that he'd had enough and simply walked offstage. He quit the emcee job.

Carey made no money until the end of that year, when he landed a one-week gig at a Pittsburgh, Pennsylvania, club called the Funny Bone. The job paid him $400. When he first took the stage, he was still worried about being heckled and driven offstage. He hadn't yet worked out a persona (public image) for his stage performance. But he was still in the Marine Reserves, so he had a buzz cut and sported the thick, black regulation-issue glasses that he is now famous for. Without even realizing it at first, Carey was drawing laughs from what the audience thought was a

A guest spot on The Tonight Show *with Johnny Carson (shown here in costume, with Ed McMahon) was long considered a stand-up comedian's ticket to fame. After a missed opportunity to appear on the show in 1989, Drew Carey was invited again in 1991.*

costume. He did add his own touch—a huge, baggy suit that he originally thought was quite stylish. Naturally, Drew assumed that audiences were laughing at his appearance, not his jokes.

One night, though, he accidently locked himself out of his bedroom and was forced to appear onstage in a normal suit and tie and wearing his "civilian" eyeglasses. The audience roared. "[P]eople busted up like I was dressed for my other act," he recalls. "I thought, '[m]an, these people are laughing at *me*.' . . . I couldn't believe it. So I realized I must be . . . a goofy-looking guy—I just had no idea up until then."

As Carey grew more popular, he also changed his stand-up material. He gradually discovered that he got bigger laughs when he peppered his language with profanity. "I started talking to the audience with the same words I used when I talked to my friends in a bar. I went from respectable laughs to belly laughs. I got more work and made more money," he says in *Dirty Jokes and Beer*. "After that, I even stopped censoring my subject matter and went before every crowd like they were all old drinking buddies, speaking as intimately as I cared to."

But Carey insists that the secret to his success wasn't the profanity itself: "Being vulgar won't get you far," he maintains. "The key was, I was being honest with the audience, and true to myself. . . . That's the best way I know how to do things." Whatever kind of language he used, though, Drew Carey continued to work on finding his own special voice and on developing the sort of material he liked best.

Many comics build acts around their own personal lives. Paul Reiser, for example, a stand-up comic and the star of television's *Mad About You*, gets laughs from talking about his real-life marriage. That premise also inspired the hit show. Drew Carey, on the other hand, approaches comedy differently. He prefers to focus on what he calls the "sacred cows" of American society, subjects and issues that most of us hold near and dear. In one act, for example, he skewers Disneyland, a favorite all-American tourist attraction in California, by describing a "do-it-yourself" vacation to the resort, which you can take without leaving home: "Drive the entire family five blocks away from home and park. Walk back home. Then walk around in a circular line for a few hours. Then walk back to the car. On the way, burn your money."

By 1987, Carey had decided that he wanted to make a living at stand-up comedy. His ultimate goal was to become a *great* comic—the best, in fact. And he was not the only Cleveland native to have such aspirations. Tim Conway, who was one of the cast members of *The Carol Burnett Show*, affectionately describes Cleveland as a "joke city." He believes that the reason so many comedians hail from Cleveland is because Northeast Ohioans are comfortable poking fun at themselves:

The people in Cleveland every so often do an article asking why people laugh at the city, and, just in case you've forgotten, they provide you with a list, reminding people that the river caught on fire, that the mayor set his hair on fire, that they once dropped baseballs from the top of the Terminal Tower, and if you caught one you got a season's pass to Indians games, but nobody figured out that the balls would be moving at 11,000 miles an hour.

By the late 1980s, Drew Carey had become what is known in the business as a "road warrior." In other words, he began to travel the comedy circuit, going from town to town in his old station wagon to do gigs at various clubs.

Though this kind of life may sound exciting and adventurous, just about any comic who has experienced it will tell you otherwise. Life on the road is often grueling and disheartening, and Drew had a very difficult time. For about a year, he lived in his car. His old demons—feelings of worthlessness and anger—began to haunt him again. "I was miserable. I was depressed and angry all the time," he says of this period. One reason for his low spirits was that he missed his steady girlfriend, Jackie Tough, whom he'd met and fallen in love with in Cleveland in 1988.

What kept him going was his belief that he would someday reach the top of his field. That meant appearing on *The Tonight Show* with Johnny Carson. "I had no doubts I could make that happen," he says. But to reach that milestone, he had to make a name for himself in the comedy business. And that meant appearing in as many clubs as possible across the country.

As a result of his traveling, Drew was invited to appear on *Star Search*, a nationally televised show hosted by Johnny Carson's sidekick, Ed McMahon, which showcased new talent in a number of fields. Aspiring actors, singers, or comedians competed with one another for the chance to appear the following week against another challenger. Drew Carey won on his first try. But when he came back the second week, he lost.

Ed McMahon, the host of Star Search *and sidekick of* Tonight Show *host Johnny Carson. Drew Carey appeared on McMahon's talent show in 1987.*

Drew knew that the next step to making it big was to succeed in Los Angeles, California. He and Jackie rented a U-Haul, packed up their belongings, and headed for the West Coast, where they lived temporarily in a small, shabby apartment with an old friend of Drew's. Their new address may have been Hollywood, California, but it was far from glamorous.

Carey now began making the rounds of the Los Angeles comedy clubs. Eventually, he landed a gig in the most famous area club, the L.A. Improv, where top-notch comedians like Paul Reiser, Jerry Seinfeld, and Bill Maher performed. Though Drew's act was a hit, he was an outsider compared to the big names that appeared there, and he needed to prove himself before he would be accepted as a fellow comedian.

Although Jackie remembers Drew as a loving and considerate boyfriend, the pressure of leaving everything behind in his beloved hometown, trying to establish a new career, and being flat broke at the same time made Drew restless and edgy. After Drew hit the road again in 1989, their relationship began to sour, and they broke up later that year. A few years later, Drew and Jackie would briefly get back together, but soon realized that outside pressures weren't the only problems in their relationship. They remain friends today.

Carey's 1989 road trip was fairly successful, with one major exception. While he was on the road, a booking agent from *The Tonight Show* phoned him with an invitation to appear on the program. By the time Carey received the message from his answering service a few days later, it was too late for him to get back to Los Angeles in time to make that night's show. To his heartfelt disappointment, the agent informed him that they'd found someone else.

Carey may have been devastated by this close brush with fame, but he chose to treat it as a good omen instead. He fully believed that one day *The Tonight Show* would call back, and to prepare for that day he began working harder than ever. He spent hours writing and rewriting material. He accepted as many gigs as he could get. Before long, Drew Carey's hard work would pay off.

In 1991, *The Tonight Show* called again, and this time Carey was ready. He absolutely shone in his November appearance. Carson enjoyed Carey's act so much that he invited him to sit down and talk before he left the stage.

The pressure of appearing on the prestigious *Tonight Show* has left many a guest tongue-tied—especially comics, who may find themselves at a loss when asked to make conversation rather than simply deliver their practiced material. But Drew Carey felt great sitting on that couch across from his host. He made funny chitchat with Johnny Carson and Ed McMahon, whom he'd met on *Star Search*. Carey's November 1991 appearance wouldn't be his last. In fact, years later, Johnny Carson paid tribute to Drew Carey's talent when he included the comedian's first performance on his video collection, *The Best of Carson*.

Drew's TV gig did the trick. Offers for stand-up performances onstage and on television began pouring in. The Showtime cable network signed him up to write and star in two comedy specials: *Full Frontal Comedy* and *Drew Carey, Human Cartoon*, for which Carey won a Cable Ace Award. In 1993, he was nominated for another Cable Ace Award. He appeared in HBO's *14th Annual Young Comedians Show* and *Comic Strip Live*. MTV signed him up for its *1/2 Hour Comedy Hour, Comics Only*, and *Hot Country Nights*.

Carey had also been looking into an acting career and had made a guest appearance on a short-lived TV show called *The Torkelsons* in 1992. The following year, he had a small role as a taxicab passenger in the movie *The Coneheads*.

By now he had every reason to believe that he was going to enjoy lasting success as a stand-up comic. On the road, he was now a "headliner" (the talent whose name appears at the top of the bill) at most comedy clubs, and he was not only playing to much larger audiences but also earning more money than ever. He opened for Jermaine Jackson and for the Marshall Tucker Band in huge sports arenas, and he was booked in one of the biggest show-biz cities in the country, Las Vegas. Along the way, he'd made numerous friends and acquaintances with whom he is still in touch today. Drew Carey's troubles seemed to be behind him at last.

Drew dons formal attire in November 1996.

5

SITCOM STAR

CAREY'S FIRST FORAY into television was not exactly a smash hit. He was approached by Disney and producer/writer Michael Jacobs to star in a pilot for a sitcom called *Akron Man*. The program never reached the air. "[It] was a total disaster," says Carey. "The script was terrible, [and] I thought the executive producer was a total [jerk]." Carey was fired.

Within the year, however, he was offered a role in another show called *The Good Life*. NBC executives were trying to develop programs with Disney, who had a comedian named John Caponera under contract. Producers/writers Jeff Martin and Kevin Curran, who had received Emmy Awards for their previous work on programs such as *The Late Show with David Letterman* and *The Simpsons*, were called in to forge a sitcom featuring Caponera.

Then someone at Disney happened to watch *The Best of Carson* videotape and caught Drew's first appearance on *The Tonight Show*. Disney suggested that Martin and Curran contact Carey. After watching the video themselves, the two producers met with Drew. It didn't take them long to hire him as Caponera's friend on *The Good Life*.

Caponera played a character named John Bowman, a middle-class married man with three kids, who worked as a warehouse manager for the Honest Abe Security Company. Carey played his friend and coworker, Drew (the character borrowed Carey's first name). Drew says that the producers "picked the security company because they were looking to have our characters in the most boring job they could find and that's the one that came to mind."

Drew Carey greatly enjoyed working on the set of *The Good Life*. Martin and Curran, the producers, were experienced and professional. Neither the studio nor the network gave Carey any trouble. Drew and Caponera were good friends—they'd met years before when they were both traveling the comedy club circuit—and Caponera was very easy to work with. He was a generous comic who didn't mind sharing the limelight with other cast members.

Carey worked hard at his job, not only rehearsing and acting but also contributing to the show's development by offering suggestions about his own character. He also put in a great number of hours promoting the show, filming promotional spots, and giving interviews to journalists and reporters.

The Good Life premiered in January 1994. But because it was a midseason replacement show and was scheduled at 8:30 on Tuesday nights, directly opposite the immensely popular ABC show *Home Improvement*, it never did well in the ratings. The program was also hampered by its lead-in, *Saved by the Bell*, and by the show that followed it, *The Mommies*, neither of which was successful.

Drew Carey hated *The Mommies*, a sitcom that centered around the domestic lives of two women played by housewives-turned-comics Marilyn Kentz and Caryl Kristensen. He made no attempt to disguise his feelings. In a very public moment—a press conference with the cast of *The Good Life*—Carey announced:

The Mommies is among the worst, the most pandering, insulting shows to women I've even seen on television. . . . I apologize to the executives [of NBC], but it just seems so unfair to me. I know so many, so *many*, female comics that are so funny and really deserve a break and have really been working hard. . . . But the network goes and gets these two housewives out of nowhere and gives them this thing and I don't think they deserve it.

Carey with costars John Caponera and Eve Gordon from the unsuccessful TV program The Good Life.

Unfortunately for the outspoken Drew Carey and his colleagues, even *The Mommies* lasted longer than *The Good Life*, which was canceled in April 1994, only four months after its premiere. But Drew managed to emerge professionally unscathed from the disaster. Some critics, in fact, considered him the show's only saving grace.

Most aspiring comics believe that putting in time doing stand-up is the best way to land a successful television career, but Drew Carey has never been a typical comic.

David Duchovny and Gillian Anderson as Fox Mulder and Dana Scully in the hit TV series The X-Files. *Drew Carey prefers such dramas over most of the sitcoms on television today.*

Instead, he believes exactly the opposite: that TV success will enhance his stand-up career. So even though *The Good Life* was canceled, he was not about to give up on television. "If you try to tailor your act as a sitcom audition, the act will suffer," Drew says. "If [comics] are honest with themselves, if they're smart stand-up comics, they'll do whatever they want to do . . . to make it honest and worry about the sitcom stuff later."

A taste of television work was all Drew needed to convince himself that he should have a show of his own. But once again, he was not about to travel the usual path to get one. He wanted to have control over the situation, to be able to choose his own producer and create his own show, rather than hope for an offer from someone who might have caught his act on *The Good Life*.

Drew Carey knew what he wanted. He needed a producer who believed in his brand of comedy and wouldn't try to alter it. He also wanted someone with whom he could speak frankly, and who would in turn tell him the absolute truth about his chances at success. With these qualities in mind, he launched a search for "his" producer.

Eventually he found Bruce Helford, and the two worked out the concept for a new sitcom starring a character much like Drew himself. Carey and Helford decided to base the comedy on an "alternate" Drew Carey, the person he might have been had he not become a comedian.

After deciding what the "TV Drew" would do for a living, where he would make his home, and who his friends would be, Carey and Helford pitched the idea to Warner Bros. Studios, who expressed interest in producing the series.

With Warner Bros. on board, all that Carey and Helford needed was a network willing to buy *The Drew Carey Show*. They made appointments to meet with executives from ABC, Fox, and CBS, but ABC liked the concept so much that it asked Carey and Helford to cancel their meetings with the other two networks. They wanted to buy the series immediately.

Helford and Carey began working on the pilot of *The Drew Carey Show*. (A pilot is a one-time TV program that appears before the premiere of a new series in order to gauge viewer interest in the show.) From the beginning, Carey wanted to do more than just act. He also wanted to participate in the creative aspects of the show. Although some stars (Roseanne, for example), have claimed they wrote their shows single-handedly, it is virtually impossible for the star of a program to do so.

Carey agreed to be the supervising producer of *The Drew Carey Show*. Not only does he help to write scripts, but he also works with set decorators, wardrobe designers, and other production staff members to ensure that each episode runs smoothly.

Interestingly, Drew Carey has never been a big fan of TV sitcoms. He prefers to watch news, sports programs, and investigative shows like *The X-Files*, *Homicide*, and *NYPD Blue*. He also watches the smash hit *The Simpsons*, which, like *The Drew Carey Show* itself, takes an irreverent attitude toward American society. Carey says that when he landed a spot on *The Good Life*, he tried to watch other sitcoms to get a feel for what TV comedy was like, but none of them held his interest for long. "I think they suck," he says with characteristic frankness. "I gotta tell you the truth. I really think a lot of them are horrid and I can't stand to watch them. There."

When Drew began working with Bruce Helford on *The Drew Carey Show*, however, Helford suggested that Carey get a feel for scriptwriting by helping him with an episode of *Someone Like Me*, a show that Helford was producing for NBC. The experience was an eye-opener for Carey. He gained respect for scriptwriters and began to understand how important good writing is to the success of a show.

When *The Drew Carey Show* premiered in September 1995, the regular cast members were Carey, Diedrich Bader as Oswald, Ryan Stiles as Lewis, and Christa Miller as Kate. Mimi, the acid-tongued, heavily made-up, and gaudily dressed coworker who would become Carey's archenemy, appeared in the pilot, but Carey and Helford thought that would be her only appearance.

The premise of *The Drew Carey Show* has remained intact since its pilot episode: a low-level executive has worked at a Cleveland department store for seven years. It seems unlikely that he'll ever get much of a promotion or a raise. After work, he hangs out with his friends, either at the local bar or at his home, the same house where he grew up.

Drew Carey and Christa Miller relax on TV Drew's outside sofa on the set of The Drew Carey Show. *Carey and Miller share a warm relationship both on-and off-camera.*

Even Drew's sets for the show were based on his real life. For example, in the backyard of the television house is a pool table, just like the one his father bought but his mother wouldn't allow inside the Carey house. For a personal touch, Drew added sports memorabilia from his favorite Cleveland teams. On the TV Drew's office desk is a Macintosh computer, Drew Carey's own choice in real life—but it doesn't have the Macintosh logo.

Carey even chose the show's theme song, "Moon Over Parma," a humorous song written by a Cleveland native about love in the suburbs of that city. And Drew recorded the song himself, rather than hire a professional singer.

Of the eight new ABC programs that premiered in the fall of 1995, five were sitcoms like Drew's. *The Drew Carey Show* is the only one that is still on the air. This is not unusual; every year, networks cancel dozens of sitcoms, both new and established.

What was unusual was that ABC had enough confidence in *The Drew Carey Show* to give it the best time slot available, between two other popular shows, *Ellen* and *Grace Under Fire*. Because the two programs were established hits, they'd help Carey find an instant audience. But that also meant that the stakes were high: *The Drew Carey Show* had to be successful enough not only to keep its ready-made audience, but to gain viewers. And if the show flopped, it would do so very publicly, in front of millions of TV watchers.

Once the pilot of *The Drew Carey Show* was completed, Carey was so relieved and excited that he went a little wild. He got one of his nipples pierced. A month or two later, in the heat of the summer, he also shaved his head. But he forgot that he had to film promotional spots for his show, and ended up buying a toupee so that he looked the way he had during the taping of his pilot.

With the pilot ready to air, the cast and crew of *The Drew Carey Show* devoted their energy to taping 22 more episodes for the show's first season. Before long, they settled into a new and grueling work schedule. Each Wednesday, the actors received a new script and began rehearsing a new episode. That episode was then taped the following Tuesday in front of a studio audience. After three weeks of this schedule, the cast and crew took a week-long break. All told, they filmed a year's worth of episodes in eight months.

For the most part, the cast and crew of *The Drew Carey Show* enjoy working with one another. Even outsiders who have witnessed tapings describe the set's atmosphere as "casual" and "close-knit." Stiles and Bader, who play Drew's pals Lewis and Oswald, have become inseparable, even off the air. They love to clown around, especially with the studio audience while the cameras are not running. Occasionally the cast even takes a vacation together. Several times, Drew has flown everyone to Cleveland.

But since Drew Carey is not only an actor but also one of the producers of his own show, the rehearsals and taping are only part of his work schedule. He calculates that during taping weeks, he puts in about 55 to 60 hours, not including promotional appearances and interviews. He also works during "hiatus weeks" when the other actors and crew have time off, attending production meetings and working on scripts with the show's other writers.

One lesson Carey learned during the first season of *The Drew Carey Show* was that television censors would not allow him to use the bawdy language of his stand-up acts. Each time Carey and the other scriptwriters finish a first draft, they are required to send it to Neil Conrad of ABC's Broadcast Standards and Practices Department. (Networks employ their own censors in part to stem even harsher restrictions from the federal government.)

Though Carey likes and respects Conrad, who is a fellow Cleveland native, he finds working under his watchful eye very difficult at times. Every week, scripts come back with scores of notes from Conrad requesting that the writers cut back on their use of profanity or eliminate entire lines of script he deems offensive. In *Dirty Jokes and Beer*, Carey describes his surprise at the first memo he received from Conrad: "Please note the excessive use of hell and damn found on pages 4, 20, 21, 22, 28, 38, 40, and 52, and reduce this number by half."

As a result, although *The Drew Carey Show* can sometimes be ribald, the on-air version is certainly much "cleaner" than the original scripts. Somehow, though, Drew Carey's cynical humor is never completely suppressed. By the end of its first season, *The Drew Carey Show* may not have been a ratings hit, but it clearly bore the mark of its creator's personality.

"Mr. Cleveland" himself: Drew in 1997.

6

"CLEVELAND ROCKS"

THE DREW CAREY SHOW finished its first season ranked 44th out of about 150 television programs on the Nielsen ratings chart—not exactly a stellar debut for a new sitcom. But the show had definitely won an audience, and plenty of advertisers were willing to buy commercial time during its slot. Moreoever, it managed to hold its own during a season of dismal failures for ABC. The minor success of *The Drew Carey Show* held more weight than it might have during one of the network's more prosperous seasons.

Other signs that the show was on its way to the top began to appear. In May 1996, *TV Guide* featured *The Drew Carey Show* on a list called "Bring Back These Shows." That same year, Drew Carey (along with comic Jeff Foxworthy) received a People's Choice award for Favorite New Sitcom Star. For these reasons, ABC decided that *The Drew Carey Show* deserved another chance, and signed on with Warner Bros. for another 24 episodes (a year's worth of shows).

Some of the early reviews of *The Drew Carey Show* labeled it a clone of the popular NBC sitcom *Friends*, which had premiered a year

Drew Carey likes the popular sitcom Friends, *but he does not think that his show can be compared to it.* "Gilligan's Island *was more like Friends than we were,*" *he joked after* The Drew Carey Show *premiered.*

earlier, in September 1994. Drew Carey likes *Friends*. He thinks it's well-written, well-acted, and funny. But he wasn't very happy about being compared to it. To him, being called a clone implied that his own concept wasn't original. Besides, his goal had been to create a show along the lines of *Grace Under Fire* or *Roseanne*, programs that focus on the everyday lives of middle-class people and not, as Drew puts it, on cosmopolitan characters who live "way better than they can afford to in real life."

But Carey need not have worried. The viewers who tuned in to *The Drew Carey Show* knew that they weren't watching a *Friends* knock-off. *TV Guide* called Carey himself a "refreshing middle-American alternative to TV's fixation on big-city types." And critic David Vermillion acknowledged that although the show had its rough spots, it was different from *Friends*-type programs: "If you don't know anybody as hip, cool, and sexy as the beautiful people on NBC's hit *Friends* (and who does?), then comedian Drew Carey's new sitcom is for you," he wrote. "Set in unhip Cleveland, this half-hour comedy centers around four lifelong buddies who sweat through life's everyday hassles."

Even before the second season began, the gamble ABC had taken in signing on *The Drew Carey Show* for another year seemed likely to pay off. Reruns of the show, which aired during the summer, picked up a lot of viewers who had missed it during the regular season and were looking for something different to watch. By the time the new season's episodes began airing in September 1996, *The Drew Carey Show* had become one of TV's top 20 programs, according to Nielsen ratings.

For ABC, Drew Carey, and rest of the program's cast and crew, this was very good news. Members of the television industry generally regard the 20 highest-ranking shows as bona fide hits. These shows invariably run during the period known as prime time—weekday evenings—and generate the greatest amount of advertising money per commercial spot.

The good news got even better. Unlike some other shows that hit the Top 20 only to slide back down the ratings scale, *The Drew Carey Show* maintained, and at times surpassed, its rating of 17. Midway through its third season, for example, Nielsen ranked *The Drew Carey Show* 11th out of all television shows broadcast in the United States. That meant that it was watched in 12.2 million homes that week, and presumably by more than one person in each household. The Neilsen ranking put *The Drew Carey Show* fourth on ABC's list of its most popular programs for 1997. Only the perennial favorite, *Monday Night Football*; its lead-in, the *NFL Monday Showcase*; and *Home Improvement* ranked higher.

By this time, of course, *The Drew Carey Show* was receiving regular media coverage. At the end of the 1996–97 season, the cast was featured on the cover of the popular magazine *Entertainment Weekly*, topping its list of the best shows on television.

When it became evident that *The Drew Carey Show* had enough energy to run for several seasons, Warner Bros. exercised its option to sell syndication rights to the program. In general, this means that after 100 episodes of a show (about four years' worth of new programming), individual TV stations who purchase syndication rights are permitted to air reruns of the program at any time on their own schedules.

Selling a program's syndication rights creates a huge financial windfall for the studio that produces the show. It also means that cast members continue to receive paychecks even after the program goes off the air, as long as local stations pick it up. For the cast of *The Drew Carey Show*, being put into syndication was a lucky break: this happens for only 10 percent of television shows.

By far one of the most widely recognized reasons for the success of *The Drew Carey Show* is the relationship between Carey's character and a coworker named Mimi Bobeck. Mimi was originally intended to be a marginal character whose appearance in later episodes depended on her success in the pilot. But audience reaction to her was so overwhelmingly enthusiastic that about midway through the first season of *The Drew Carey Show* she began making regular appearances. Some might think this is a curious phenomenon, since Mimi could well be the meanest, most spiteful character ever to appear on a sitcom. (One public opinion poll identified Mimi as one of the laziest characters on American television, ranking with Norm Petersen of the former show *Cheers* and Homer Simpson of the animated program *The Simpsons*.)

Calling Mimi unusual is an understatement. Her most striking feature is her outrageously garish makeup. Kathy Kinney, the actress who plays Mimi, says her character's purse contains at least five shades of blue eye shadow, a bottle of black liquid eyeliner, false eyelashes, bright scar-

Kathy Kinney as Drew's garishly dressed coworker on The Drew Carey Show. *Much of the sitcom's humor is built on the antagonistic relationship between Drew and Mimi. The TV Drew's arch-rival is so popular that Carey devoted a chapter to Mimi in his book* Dirty Jokes and Beer.

let blush, and scores of lipsticks, all of them bright red. After each taping, Kinney says she has to use handfuls of premoistened baby wipes to remove her makeup. But Mimi doesn't stop at cosmetics. She also teases her hair into a bouffant and makes a point of dressing in eye-popping neon colors, loud patterns, frills, fringes, bows, and sequins. Kinney helps the crew pick out Mimi's clothes. "[I]t's so much fun," Kinney told one magazine interview-

Kathy Kinney removes her Mimi makeup to appear with Drew at the Take a Chance with Stars cancer benefit in November 1996.

er. "It's like playing dress-up. The producers will say, 'We want Mimi to wear a skirt,' so I'll suggest a poodle skirt and we'll keep going until we have another whole new wacky Mimi outfit."

Mimi is such an outlandish character that many viewers tune in to *The Drew Carey Show* especially to see her—or, more accurately, her interactions with her archenemy, Drew. Kinney remembers the very simple act by which she turned Mimi into Drew's nemesis: in the show's second episode, she says, the script called for Mimi to hand an envelope to Drew. "[A]s soon as I started to hand it to him I decided to cough on it," she says. "In that moment, Mimi was born."

Since then, Mimi and Drew have delighted in putting

each other down and pulling pranks on one another. Some plots even call for one of them to plan the other's ultimate downfall. In one episode, for example, they tried to get one another arrested for stealing from the department store where they work.

In keeping with her physical appearance, Mimi's most popular lines are insults. To the dismay of some people who are not followers of *The Drew Carey Show*, phrases like "Hi, pig" (Mimi's customary greeting for Drew) and "Bite me!" (her response to just about any perceived threat) have been adopted by *Drew Carey Show* fans across the country.

Mimi may be hard to miss, but Kathy Kinney is a quiet, subdued person. In his book, Carey describes her as "the total opposite of the character she plays on TV. She's one of the nicest people I've ever met, never raising her voice or showing any signs of bad temper. Ever." Nor does she dress like her TV counterpart. "She rarely wears makeup," Drew says, "and if she does, she wears very little. Also, she never dresses in any wild clothes." And Carey calls his costar "a total professional, never blowing a line or failing to deliver a joke."

Thanks to the success of her Mimi character, Kathy Kinney now gets tons of fan mail. In a feature article in *People* magazine, Kinney said that she hears from people from all across the country and from all walks of life. But Mimi has also received attention from sources outside the entertainment industry. When *Personnel Journal*, a professional magazine, published an article about discrimination against employees based on their appearance, the piece began with a discussion of Mimi. In August 1997, *American Business Review* ran an article on the cosmetics industry entitled "Mimi's 'Look' Gives Cosmetics a Bad Name."

With all this publicity, positive and otherwise, Carey and his costars appeared to be on a roll as *The Drew Carey Show* began its second season in September 1996. To top off the success, later in the season ABC moved the show

Hometown boy: sporting an Indians baseball cap and jersey, Carey throws out the first pitch at the Cleveland Indians' home opener against the Anaheim Angels in April 1998.

from 8:30 P.M. (7:30 P.M. in Central and Pacific time zones) to 9:00 Eastern time. The earlier slot is considered part of prime-time's "family hour," when more children may be watching than at later hours, and censors tend to be more strict about the language and content of shows airing during that time. The half-hour switch made a big difference to Carey and his cowriters, who felt that they could now include material that was a bit more adult.

By the time *The Drew Carey Show* entered its third season in the fall of 1997, the characters had become clearly defined, the scripts were smoother, and even Drew Carey himself was earning praise for what was once called "wooden" acting. But the program has never lost its brash attitude. One aspect of the show that set it apart from nearly every other program on the air at the time was its unusual opening: a full dance number that included all of the show's cast members. To the theme song "Cleveland Rocks" (performed by the group the Presidents of the United States of America), Carey, his costars, and 3,000 residents of Cleveland seemingly danced across the city, in front of local landmarks such as the Rock and Roll Hall of Fame and the Hope Memorial Bridge. The extravaganza ended when Carey shouted "Ohio!" at the close of the song.

The fame of *The Drew Carey Show* has even reached cyberspace. Fans have demonstrated their dedication with scores of web pages, where visitors can catch up on the latest episodes of the show, read material relating to its stars, and view photos and bits of information posted by other fans. One site features a weekly interactive trivia quiz. At the end of 1997, another site boasted more than 45,000 "hits" (the number of visitors to a site). The page is one of a ring of Drew Carey websites that are connected to one another by links.

Observers of the Drew Carey phenomenon have often compared its premise to that of cartoonist Scott Adams, the creator of the "Dilbert" comic strip, which also focuses on a group of put-upon office workers and their day-to-day problems. The "Dilbert" strip seems to have taken the nine-to-five working world by storm: one would be hard-pressed to find an office in America where at least one "Dilbert" comic strip wasn't in evidence on a bulletin board. So when Adams noticed that the TV Drew had taped a "Dilbert" cartoon to his cubicle, he made note of it in his own newsletter. Was Carey a "Dilbert" fan? Adams wondered publicly. If not, perhaps he should be placed on Adams's Enemies List.

In reply, Drew Carey sent an E-mail to Adams, asking that the cartoonist refrain from listing him as an enemy. He offered to place a few "Dilbert" mementos on the set. Sure enough, not long after the exchange between the comic and the cartoonist, Dilbert and Dogbert dolls (Dogbert is the character's sidekick) appeared as props on *The Drew Carey Show*. In exchange, Adams would have Dilbert and Dogbert playing on an outdoor pool table—a reference to the set of Drew's program.

As might be expected, *The Drew Carey Show* has received a great deal of media coverage in Ohio, especially in Cleveland. The success of the show has been a considerable source of pride for many of the city's residents, who revel in the small but significant homages Drew Carey pays to his hometown. In addition to choosing a local musician's tune for the first season's theme song, Carey often wears and uses Cleveland memorabilia on the show, such as a T-shirt bearing the image of a horror-movie host on a local TV channel, or a mug with the Cleveland Clinic logo on it. Carey loves Cleveland sports teams, too, but when the owner of the Cleveland Browns announced that the team was moving to Baltimore, Maryland, Carey removed all the Browns memorabilia from his set.

Drew Carey is not the only actor to benefit from the success of his show. Except for Kathy Kinney, Drew's costars were all veteran actors who had yet to make names for themselves. It seems likely that *The Drew Carey Show* is the "big break" they were all working toward.

The show's success also depends on many people working behind the scenes. Watch the credits of any television show and you will realize how much work goes into each episode. Carey is well aware of this fact: in *Dirty Jokes and Beer*, he describes the tremendous amount of effort that goes into making a popular television show. He tells his readers about some of the vital off-camera employees on every TV sound stage, such as the "grip" (the set's handyman or jack-of-all-trades), a transportation captain (the person who drives the equipment to and from a set), and a Foley artist (the person in charge of sound effects).

But the ever-sarcastic Drew Carey doesn't let it go at that. In the acknowledgements for *Dirty Jokes and Beer*, he humorously lists the other people who are making money from his own success. He thanks two managers, a lawyer, all of his talent agents, an accountant, two publicists, a literary agent, and his own assistant. Over the years, Carey says, he will provide them all with steady employment.

Drew stoops to a bit of shameless advertising at the 54th Annual Golden Globe Awards in 1997.

7

FAME AND FORTUNE

DREW CAREY READILY admits that being in show business has disadvantages as well as benefits. In *Dirty Jokes and Beer*, he says that nearly everyone has some kind of experience that is similar to what one goes through to become a star.

Carey likens show business to "high school with money." And since most adults have attended high school, he reasons, "everything that I've experienced being a TV star, most of you have experienced yourself." He goes on:

> Ever been gossiped about at school (or at work)? You know what it's like to be in the tabloids. Ever been in a popular clique? An unpopular one? You know what it's like to work on a hit show, or one that's failing. . . . Ever gotten married? Was it a big wedding? Hey, welcome to being a celebrity! You know what it's like to have people you don't even know look at you funny all day long. . . . Every day is like that. I can't take off the stupid wedding dress.

Of course, there are also aspects of stardom that Drew loves. The most obvious is the pay, which he calls "ridiculous." He admits that,

Comedian Jeff Foxworthy and Drew Carey share the 1996 People's Choice Award for Favorite Male Actor in a New Television Series.

like many others, he once complained about the amazingly high salaries American sports figures earn annually. But "[you'll] never hear me complaining about an overpaid sports star again," he remarks. Not that he's changed his mind on the subject. He's just discovered that, given the opportunity, he has also chosen to take advantage of the financial benefits of being a celebrity.

A 1996 television industry article reported that during the previous year, each member of the *Friends* cast earned $40,000 per episode. John Lithgow, the star of *Third Rock from the Sun*, made $75,000 per episode. Tim Allen of *Home Improvement* earned $200,000, while Kelsey Grammer (*Frazier*) took in $250,000 for each new episode. And comedian Bill Cosby, a veteran TV star, earned $1 million for every episode of his new program, *Cosby*.

Even if Drew Carey is earning a relatively low salary, he is also paid a significant sum to act as producer and scriptwriter for his show. But for the most part, Drew Carey has escaped the criticism usually aimed at highly paid celebrities, perhaps because he has yet to make an issue of his salary. While several television stars, including the cast of *Friends*, went on strike in an effort to negotiate better contracts for themselves, Drew Carey claimed to be perfectly happy with the stipulations of his original contract. In the August 1996 *Entertainment Weekly* article, Carey was praised for his even-tempered reaction to the great salary debate. "I get a regular 5 percent bump [each year], and I'm happy with that. But when I'm No. 1," he joked, "BA-BOOM!"

Drew Carey will also make millions from the sale of syndication rights to *The Drew Carey Show*. He occasionally earns a nice handful of money making "cameo," or one-time, appearances on other TV shows, such as *Home Improvement*, *Lois & Clark: The New Adventures of Superman*, *Dharma and Greg*, and *Sabrina, the Teenage Witch*, in addition to such oddball comedy shows as *The George Carlin Show* and *Weird Al*. And true to his original goal, Carey still performs his stand-up act whenever he has time, either in comedy clubs or at gatherings like annual corporate meetings.

The success of *The Drew Carey Show* has also opened up new television opportunities for Carey. In August 1998, ABC premiered a new program called *Whose Line Is It, Anyway?*, co-produced and hosted by Drew. *Whose Line* is an unusual show in which improvisational comedians act out situations while an "emcee" directs the action. It was based on a British program with the same name that ran for 10 years in England and aired in reruns on the Comedy Central cable network in the United States until 1997.

Drew's version of the show features the same comics who appeared in the British program: Colin Mochrie, Greg Proops, Brad Sherwood, Wayne Brady, and Ryan Stiles (Lewis on *The Drew Carey Show*). Stiles appeared for six seasons on the British version of *Whose Line Is It, Anyway?* before he auditioned for *The Drew Carey Show*.

Then there's Drew Carey merchandise. In 1997, a book agent landed Carey a contract with the New York publisher Hyperion (which is owned by Disney) to write the autobiography that Drew eventually titled *Dirty Jokes and Beer*. Carey has laughingly claimed that he made "a zillion dollars" on the deal. The truth is, however, that the $3 million advance Hyperion paid Drew Carey made him an instant millionaire.

Most celebrity autobiographies are "ghostwritten"; that is, the celebrity makes notes and dictates ideas to a professional writer working for a fee, who then turns the material into a publishable book with the celebrity's name on the cover. In the case of stand-up comedians who are also television stars, such as Jerry Seinfeld, Paul Reiser, and Ellen DeGeneres, the books are far from autobiographical, however. Instead, they are often largely joke books that include bits and pieces of their stand-up acts.

Drew Carey wanted to write his book himself, without benefit of a ghostwriter, even though he had no writing experience. He also wanted to balance the jokes with a bit of information about his own life. He took his book contract very seriously. In typical Drew Carey fashion, he bought "a whole slew of 'how to write' books" and set out to complete the work himself.

In his introduction, Carey admits to his readers that he has done all the writing himself. "I just wanted to remind you that I didn't use a ghostwriter for this. I could have. I probably should have, it would've been easier. But because of pride I didn't." He admits that he did get some input from his editors at Hyperion, and also from a few friends who "came in about five days before the deadline

Carey makes an author appearance at a bookstore in New York City to promote his 1997 book Dirty Jokes and Beer.

and helped calm me down and show me where the apostrophes are supposed to go."

Despite the book's title, it contains more than just jokes. He includes 10 humorous essays which, he wryly claims, are "for the editors and publishers at Hyperion. . . . Thanks for the cash." He also added a strictly autobiographical section where he not only discusses his own past and the difficulties he's had to overcome, but also what it feels like to be a TV star. Lastly, the reader is treated to five fictional stories, which are darkly disturbing. This section, called "Stories of the Unrefined," is a section that Drew admits "the publishers at Hyperion wish would just go away."

Dirty Jokes and Beer was so popular that it landed on *USA Today*'s list of bestsellers. But it got mixed reviews. The book is not for the faint of heart; some people find it coarse and obscene. Others see through the profanity and call it thoughtful and funny. Many believe that it is at least strikingly honest. One critic wrote, "From growing up without a dad to beefing up in the marines, Carey does not seek understanding or sympathy as much as he is sharing an unrepentant self-evaluation of the events that helped to shape his life."

Another merchandising opportunity arrived in September 1998, when toy manufacturer Creation Entertainment turned the TV Drew and his nemesis, Mimi, into Barbie-sized dolls. "We thought [*The Drew Carey Show*] would be a good show to license dolls for because Drew and Mimi are like caricatures themselves," says a spokesperson for the company. Drew Carey and Kathy Kinney were consulted to be sure that the toys resembled them in appearance, clothing, and—in Mimi's case—makeup. Carey describes the dolls simply as "cool."

For Drew Carey, making lots of money, having the chance to "become" a doll, and writing a bestselling book are a few of the biggest advantages of being a television star. But they're not the only ones. He also loves to do commercial endorsements. The Nike company, for example, which buys a great deal of advertising time during Drew's show, also sends him shoes and clothing. He's been invited to a number of exciting events, such as movie premieres and the Super Bowl. And he jokes that he is now more appealing to beautiful women and gets lots of dates.

But he sees disadvantages to stardom as well. Because of his line of work, he lives in Los Angeles, even though he really doesn't like the city at all. He greatly misses doing stand-up comedy. And like every celebrity, his fame

has cost him his privacy. Since *The Drew Carey Show* became a hit, he has found himself increasingly in the limelight, unable to find time for himself.

Despite his reputation as a wise-cracking cynic, Drew Carey is unfailingly pleasant to fans who stop him to get an autograph or to talk to him. A reporter who accompanied Carey on a visit to Cleveland remarked that he

With the Detroit Tigers mascot at his side, avid sports fan Drew Carey signs autographs for his own fans during an all-star celebrity softball game in July 1997.

seemed to genuinely enjoy shaking hands and giving out autographs. What Carey doesn't enjoy, however, is the attention he draws from magazines and other media. Like many other celebrities, he finds tabloid articles especially annoying. Magazines like the *National Enquirer* or the *Star* specialize in publishing scandalous or sensational material that is often fabricated. Carey readily admits that the tabloids have been far nicer to him than to many other celebrities. But he has no sympathy or patience for misinformation. "They lie," Drew says. "And if they don't make up a lie themselves, they'll pass on whatever lies someone else has told them."

Some of the stories reported in tabloids are relatively harmless and can be hilarious. In his book, Drew recounts an article in the *Star* that reported he had lost 17 pounds on an all-potato diet. Quoting an unnamed "pal," they attributed to him statements he'd never made and printed "before" and "after" photos in which, Drew says, he weighs exactly the same. "He's telling his costar Kathy Kinney that it could work for her. Drew is telling all his pudgy pals that it's the latest celebrity craze," the *Star* raved. Drew adds, "Never happened. Never said it. Never would say it." He says he cannot in a million years imagine himself saying, "Hey pudgy pal, this potato diet is the latest celebrity craze!"

Carey and his friends all laughed about the potato diet story. But he found another tabloid tale truly upsetting. Carey had been dating a woman who meant a great deal to him, but the relationship hadn't worked out, and they were breaking up. At the same time, a tabloid printed a story claiming that the two were secretly engaged. His former girlfriend was very hurt by the story, and both she and Drew were faced with answering questions about the supposed engagement.

Ultimately, Drew says, the tabloids worry him. He asks, "Is the cute blonde that says she wants to [date] me being paid $75,000 by *The Globe* to tape-record the encounter?

Can I throw my mail in the trash like a normal person or do I have to buy a shredder so that someone from a tabloid doesn't grab it from my garbage can?"

In many ways, Carey downplays his celebrity status. He still enjoys presenting himself as an everyman. In his book and in interviews, he still comes off as a regular guy, just like the rest of us. He still stays at inexpensive Red Roof Inns while traveling. He likes to go to places like Big Boy and Denny's, instead of expensive, gourmet restaurants. (Drew claims that it isn't because he doesn't appreciate fine food; it's because the fancy places won't let him stay at his table and read after dinner.) Drew vacations in the usual American tourist spots, like Florida or Las Vegas. And his dream car is a Ford, not a Rolls-Royce.

Even though he's recognized all over the country, Drew Carey tries hard to stay grounded. Although he doesn't mind spending time alone, he makes an effort to stay in touch with old friends. He returns as often as he can to Cleveland, where he still visits his old haunts. One day, he plans to renovate his childhood home and move back there to live.

Although most people accept Drew Carey as the "Joe Blow" he claims he is, some take issue with this characterization. After all, they say, how can he still be one of us when he's so famous and makes so much money? On the surface, perhaps they're right. But Drew Carey doesn't think so. After his television show goes off the air, he says, he's going right back to stand-up comedy. He's toyed with the idea of making a couple of movies, but what he really wants to do when he leaves television is to simply fade away from the public eye—to "take off the wedding dress," as he says, "and disappear."

CHRONOLOGY

1958   Drew Allison Carey born on May 23 in Cleveland, Ohio, to Lewis and Beulah Carey

1966   Lewis Carey dies of brain cancer; Drew begins to suffer from depression

1967   Drew is sexually molested

1975   Graduates one year early from high school; begins attending Kent State University

1976   Attempts suicide while in college

1980   Drops out of college; moves to Las Vegas, Nevada; attempts suicide a second time. After a brief stay in Cleveland, moves to San Diego, California, to live with brother Neal; joins the U.S. Marine Corps Reserve for six-year tour of duty

1985   Returns to Cleveland; begins writing jokes for morning radio program

1986   Begins emceeing and performing stand-up comedy in Cleveland

1987   Travels the stand-up comedy circuit; appears on *Star Search*

1988   Moves to Los Angeles, California

1991   Appears on *The Tonight Show*

1992   Appears in two Showtime comedy specials; wins Cable Ace Award for *Drew Carey, Human Cartoon*; appears on several HBO and MTV specials

1994   Costars with comedian John Caponera in NBC-TV sitcom *The Good Life*

1995   *The Drew Carey Show* premieres in September

1997   Publishes *Dirty Jokes and Beer*

1998   Becomes cohost and executive producer of *Whose Line Is It, Anyway?*

BIBLIOGRAPHY

Allen, Tim. *Don't Stand Too Close to a Naked Man*. New York: Hyperion, 1994.

Boyer, Paul S., et al. *Enduring Vision: A History of the American People*. Lexington, MA: D. C. Heath, 1993.

Carey, Drew. *Dirty Jokes and Beer*. New York: Hyperion, 1997.

Heldenfels, R. D., and Mark Dawidziak. "Haven't Heard Any Cleveland Jokes Lately, Have You?" *Cleveland Beacon Journal Extra*, January 26, 1997.

McDonald, Stef. "All Dolled Up." *TV Guide*, August 1, 1998.

"Mimi's 'Look' Gives Cosmetics a Bad Name," *American Business Review*, August 4, 1997.

Newman, Bruce. "Drew's Crew." *TV Guide*, August 1, 1998.

Schwed, Mark. "Kickin' Around with Drew." *TV Guide*, August 26, 1996.

"Some Words You Still Can't Say on TV." *Toronto Sun*, August 27, 1996.

Stebbins, Robert A. *The Laugh-Makers: Stand-Up Comedy as Art, Business, and Life-Style*. Montreal: McGill-Queen's University Press, 1990.

Tracy, Kathleen. *Home Brewed: The Drew Carey Story*. New York: Boulevard Books, 1997.

Watson, Brett. "Are They Worth It?" *Entertainment Weekly*, August 16, 1996.

Wolff, Jurgen, and L. P. Ferrante. *Successful Sitcom Writing*. New York: St. Martin's Press, 1996.

APPENDIX

SEXUAL ABUSE—WHERE TO GET HELP AND INFORMATION

■ BOOKS FOR PARENTS AND CHILDREN:

Bassett, Susan. *When I Go to Bed At Night: A Modern Tale of Fear, Magic, and Healing.* Redmond, WA: Enchanted Swan Productions, 1994.

Lowery, Linda. *Laurie Tells*. Minneapolis: Carolrhoda Books, 1994.

Reinert, Dale Robert. *Sexual Abuse and Incest*. Springfield, NJ: Enslow Publishers, 1997.

■ ORGANIZATIONS:

Central Agencies Sexual Abuse Treatment (CASAT)
900 Dufferin Street, Suite 201
Toronto, Ontario M6H 4B1 Canada
416-324-2425
http://www.casat.on.ca
E-mail: feedback@casat.on.ca

International Society for the Prevention of Child Abuse & Neglect (ISPCAN)
200 North Michigan Avenue,
Suite 500
Chicago, IL 60601
312-578-1401
http://child.cornell.edu/ispcan.org/
E-mail: svevo@sba.com

National Center for Missing and Exploited Children
2101 Wilson Boulevard, Suite 550
Arlington, VA 22201-3077
703-235-3900 or 800-843-5678
http://www.ncmec.org/

National Clearinghouse on Child Abuse and Neglect Information
330 C Street, S.W.
Washington, DC 20447
703-385-3206 or 800-394-3366
http://www.calib.com/nccanch/
E-mail: nccanch@calib.com

National Committee to Prevent Child Abuse, New York State
134 South Swan Street
Albany, NY 12210
800-CHILDREN (in New York)
518-445-1273
http://child.cornell.edu/ncpca/home.html
ncpcanys@aol.com

■ WEBSITES:

Canadian Society for the Investigation of Child Abuse (CSICA)
http://www.csica.zener.com/

Family Advocacy Program Online (U.S. Army)
http://child.cornell.edu/army/fap.html

DEPRESSION—WHERE TO GET HELP AND INFORMATION

■ BOOKS FOR PARENTS AND CHILDREN:

Ayer, Eleanor H. *Everything You Need to Know About Depression.* New York: Rosen Publishing Group, 1997.

Garland, E. Jane. *Depression Is the Pits, But I'm Getting Better: A Guide for Adolescents.* Washington, DC: Magination Press, 1997.

Ingersoll, Barbara, and Sam Goldstein. *Lonely, Sad and Angry.* New York: Doubleday, 1995.

Loueen, Alexander. *Depression and the Body.* New York: Penguin USA, 1993.

Newman, Susan. *Don't Be S.A.D.: A Teenage Guide to Handling Stress, Anxiety, and Depression.* New York: Julian Messner, 1991.

Wibbelsman, Charles, and Kathy McCoy. *Life Happens: A Teenager's Guide to Friends, Failure, Sexuality, Love, Rejection, Addiction, Peer Pressure, Families, Loss, Depression, Change, and Other Challenges of Living.* New York: Perigee Books, 1996.

■ ORGANIZATIONS AND WEBSITES:

American Psychiatric Association (APA)
1400 K Street, N.W.
Washington, DC 20005
202-682-6325
http://www.psych.org

American Psychological Association
750 First Street, N.E.
Washington, DC 20002-4242
202-336-5500

Children and Depression
http://members.aol.com/depress/children.htm

Depression.com
http://www.depression.com

Depression Resources List
http://www.execpc.com/~corbeau/

Foundation for Depression and Manic Depression
24 East 81st Street
New York, NY 10021
212-772-3400

National Depressive and Manic-Depressive Association
730 North Franklin Street, Suite 501
Chicago, IL 60610-3526
800-826-3632 or 312-642-0049
http://www.ndmda.org
E-mail: myrtis@aol.com

National Institute of Mental Health
5600 Fishers Lane
Room 7C-02
Bethesda, MD 20857-0001
800-443-3675
http://www.nimh.nih.gov/
E-mail: nimhinfo@nih.gov

National Mental Health Association
1021 Prince Street
Alexandria, VA 22314-2971
703-684-7722 or 800-969-NMHA

INDEX

PICTURE CREDITS

ANN GRAHAM GAINES, the author of several books for young adults, is a freelance writer who lives in Gonzales, Texas.

JAMES SCOTT BRADY serves on the board of trustees with the Center to Prevent Handgun Violence and is the Vice Chairman of the Brain Injury Foundation. Mr. Brady served as Assistant to the President and White House Press Secretary under President Ronald Reagan. He was severely injured in an assassination attempt on the president, but remained the White House Press Secretary until the end of the administration. Since leaving the White House, Mr. Brady has lobbied for stronger gun laws. In November 1993, President Bill Clinton signed the Brady Bill, a national law requiring a waiting period on handgun purchases and a background check on buyers.